The Little Book of
INSECTS

**BUSHEL
& PECK
BOOKS**

LCCN: 2022934186
ISBN: 9781638190042

First Edition

Printed in the United States

10 9 8 7 6 5 4 3 2 1

The Little Book of
INSECTS

CHRISTIN FARLEY

CONTENTS

WHAT MAKES
SOMETHING AN INSECT?

Insects—members of the class *Insecta*—all share a few common characteristics: they have a three-part body (made up of a head, thorax, and abdomen), an exoskeleton, three pairs of legs, a single pair of antennae, and compound eyes. That means that some of the creepy crawlies you might *think* are insects actually aren't. Spiders? Nope, they're arachnids. Centipedes? They're not insects either (they're arthropods). Though there are nearly ten million different insect species in the world, it turns not just anything can be called one!

In this book, you'll meet some of the world's most common types of insects. From beetles to butterflies, each plays an important role in the world around us. After all, insects are a major source of food for animals, they help pollinate plants, and they even aerate the soil. They might just be the hardest working creatures on the planet!

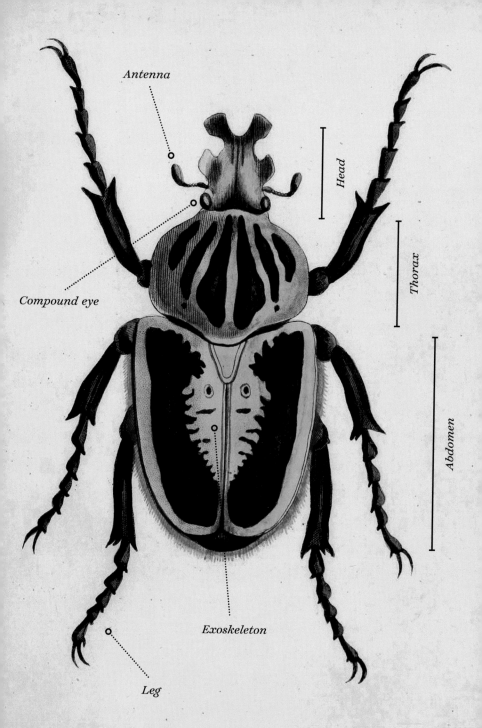

Antenna

Head

Thorax

Compound eye

Abdomen

Exoskeleton

Leg

MEET THE
INSECTS

1. BEETLE

The beetles that we see today have been around for 230 million years. They make up the largest group of living organisms on earth and are found worldwide (except for polar regions). There are three distinct features to look for when identifying a beetle. First, its wing coverings are on its back; these covers, called elytra, look like a hard shell. Next, look for chewing mouthparts, or mandibles, on the underside of its head. Yes, beetles chew their food! Lastly, beetles have six legs spread out between their front and back body segments. If you count a number other than six for legs, then your bug is not a beetle!

CLASSIFICATION

KINGDOM: *Animalia*

PHYLUM: *Arthropoda*

CLASS: *Insecta*

ORDER: *Coleoptera*

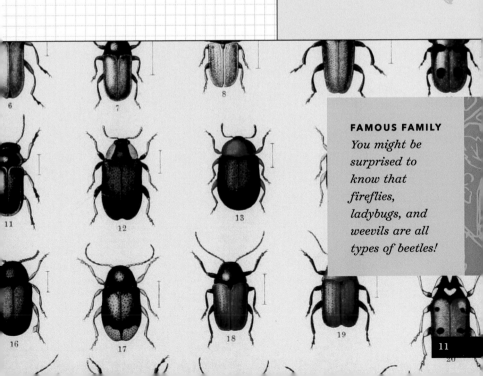

FAMOUS FAMILY
You might be surprised to know that fireflies, ladybugs, and weevils are all types of beetles!

BIG BUGS

The Amazon rainforest is the home to the largest known beetle. The Titan beetle can grow up to almost seven inches in length!

Titan
Beetle

Hercules
Beetle

SUPER STRENGTH

The Hercules beetle can lift 850 times its own body
weight. That is the equivalent of an average human
adult lifting six school buses!

Ladybug

STINKY FEAST

The dung beetle rolls dung (poop) into balls, which are then rolled underground to where they'll be fed on by the young. Tasty!

Dung
Beetle

Stag
Beetle

AND IN THE FAR CORNER . . .

The stag beetle has huge mandibles that look like the antlers of a stag. Male stag beetles use these to wrestle each other, sometimes for a mate and sometimes for a preferred food source.

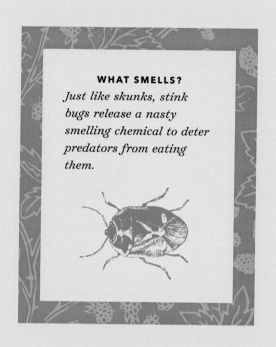

WHAT SMELLS?

Just like skunks, stink bugs release a nasty smelling chemical to deter predators from eating them.

Stink
Bug

NOW THAT'S A LOT OF BUGS

Scientists have discovered over 350,000 species of beetles, though it's thought that up to 3 million species are living. Most have not yet been discovered.

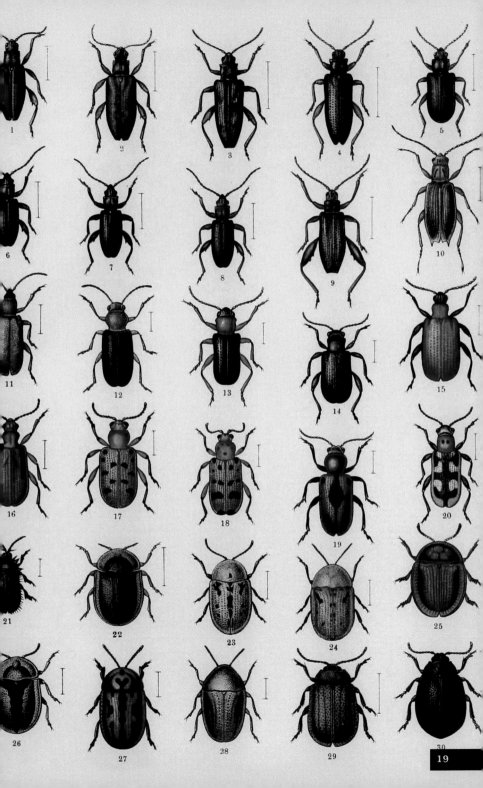

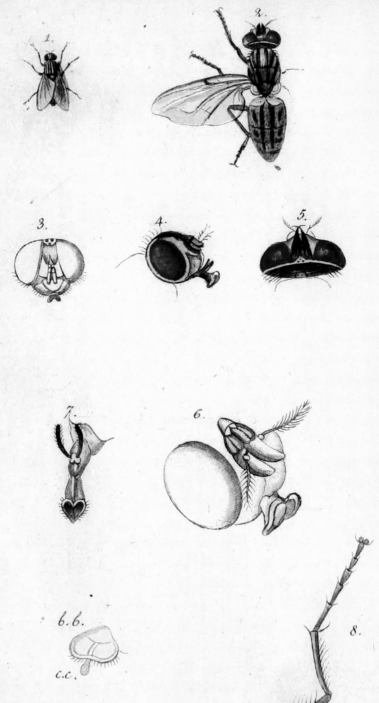

Housefly

2. FLY

Flies belong to one of the largest insect orders called *Dipteran*. Though there are many insects that are called flies, *true* flies are two-winged, not four-winged like other insects. These interesting eaters vomit an acidic substance on their food that turns it into liquid. Since flies don't chew, they suck up their liquified food with a long tongue structure. Though known for their pesky buzzing and constant defecating, flies are surprisingly beneficial to humans. With over 120,000 species worldwide, flies provide an important source of food for animals like snakes, frogs, and birds. They are also part of the earth's clean-up crew because they feed on decaying matter. A fly's average lifespan is around twenty-eight days.

KINGDOM: *Animalia*

PHYLUM: *Arthropoda*

CLASS: *Insecta*

SUPERORDER: *Panorpida*

ORDER: *Diptera*

Horse-Fly

SPEED DEMON

The fastest flying insect is the horse-fly, which can reach top speeds of ninety miles per hour!

21

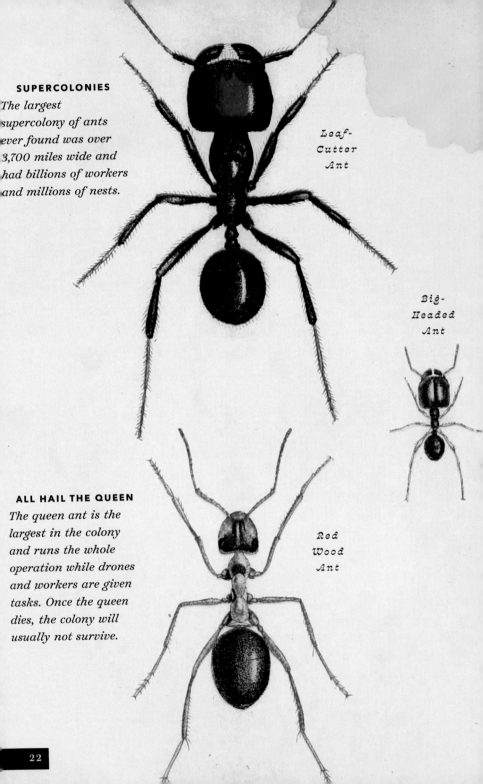

SUPERCOLONIES
*The largest
supercolony of ants
ever found was over
3,700 miles wide and
had billions of workers
and millions of nests.*

Leaf-
Cutter
Ant

Big-
Headed
Ant

ALL HAIL THE QUEEN
*The queen ant is the
largest in the colony
and runs the whole
operation while drones
and workers are given
tasks. Once the queen
dies, the colony will
usually not survive.*

Red
Wood
Ant

3. ANT

Ants are not just found at picnics; they live all over the world! These amazing insects make up over 12,000 species, and all them have a tough, waterproof exoskeleton and the ability to lift at least twenty times their own body weight. While they don't have ears or lungs, they can sense the world around them through vibrations. Tiny holes in their bodies allow for the exchange of oxygen and carbon dioxide. Social creatures, ants live in colonies where they work together for the good of the group. And did you know? Each ant has two stomachs: one to hold its own food, and a second to store food to bring back home to support ants who are working in the nest.

CLASSIFICATION

KINGDOM: *Animalia*

PHYLUM: *Arthropoda*

CLASS: *Insecta*

ORDER: *Hymenoptera*

INFRAORDER: *Aculeata*

SUPERFAMILY: *Formicoidea*

FAMILY: *Formicidae*

A PAINFUL POKE

In the jungles of the Amazon lives the bullet ant, which is said to have the most painful sting in the world. Some have compared it to being hit by a bullet. Ouch!

4. BEE

You can hear the familiar buzzing of bees—over 20,000 species of them!—on any non-arctic continent. These furry insects vary in size, from the super small at two millimeters in length to the super large at one and a half inches in length. Only one type of bee makes honey, and that's the honeybee. But all bees play a vital role in keeping ecosystems healthy. That's because a bee spends nearly all its time collecting pollen and nectar from flowers. Pollen is collected on their legs, while nectar is sucked up with a straw-like mouth and stored in a sac called a crop. Thanks to bees carrying pollen from one flower to the next, plants get pollinated and food is able to grow. We couldn't survive without them!

7.   9.

RUN LIKE THE WIND
Africanized bees, or "killer bees" as they're somtimes called, are a hybrid form of honeybees that are aggressive and can swarm and attack both humans and animals. These bees have been known to chase a person up to a quarter of a mile!

*Honeybees are the most
common type of bee
and are the only insect
that directly produces
food for humans. They
need to visit two million
flowers to create just
one pound of honey.*

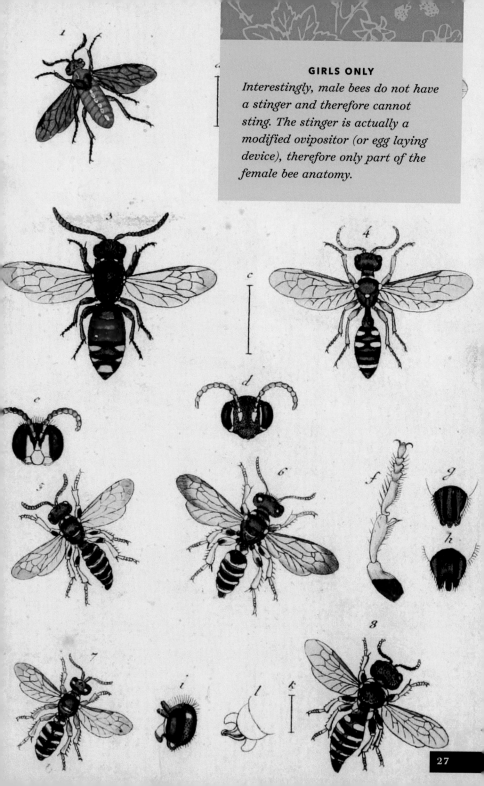

WHAT A WINGSPAN

Birdwing butterflies (like those shown here) include some of the largest butterfly species in the world! The largest living butterfly, the Queen Alexandra birdwing (not shown), has an impressive wingspan of almost twelve inches. This rare beauty is only found in the New Guinea rainforests.

5. BUTTERFLY

Butterflies are graceful fliers that come in a wide array of colors. With over 20,000 species, you are bound to find a favorite! Not just known for their beauty, butterflies are also hardworking pollinators who accomplish a lot in the few weeks they live. One of the more fragile insects, a butterfly's best protection against predators is its wings. Bright wing colors make them appear toxic to enemies, while some exhibit clever camouflage patterns that help butterflies blend in. Speaking of wings, if you take a closer look, you will see that butterflies have four wings instead of two. They take flight by moving each side's set in a figure-eight motion.

KINGDOM: *Animalia*

PHYLUM: *Arthropoda*

CLASS: *Insecta*

ORDER: *Lepidoptera*

SUBORDER: *Rhopalocera*

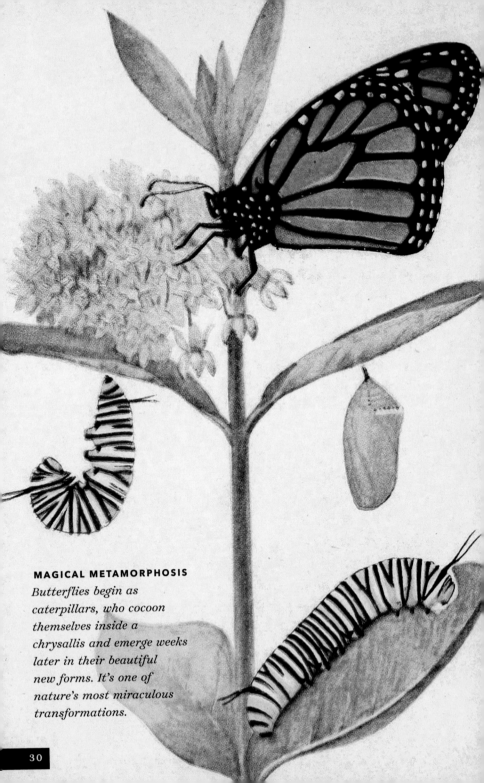

MAGICAL METAMORPHOSIS

*Butterflies begin as
caterpillars, who cocoon
themselves inside a
chrysallis and emerge weeks
later in their beautiful
new forms. It's one of
nature's most miraculous
transformations.*

30

CRAZY COLORS

Caterpillars come in so many colors and patterns. Some are wooly, some are smooth, some have spots, some have stripes, and some even have "eyes" on their rear end!

CAN'T SEE ME

Many butterflies have excellent camouflage to hide from predators. The orange oakleaf, like the butterflies to the left, looks just like a regular old leaf. The owl butterfly, shown below, keeps predators away with large spots that look like giant owl eyes!

A

FEET FOODIES

Butterflies taste with their feet. Before the female lays her eggs on a leaf, she tastes the leaf to make sure it will be a suitable food source for her caterpillar kids.

TIRELESS TRAVELERS
The well-known monarch butterfly will migrate thousands of miles from the eastern United States to Mexico in the winter.

6. MOTH

Moths are are related to butterflies, as both belong to the *Lepidoptera* order. Like butterflies, moths come in a variety of colors, shapes, and sizes. For every butterfly, there are nine moths! One of the key differences between the two is that moths tend to rest with their wings open, while butterflies generally close their wings while resting. With over 160,000 species, moths can be found worldwide. Moths are generally considered agricultural pests because their caterpillars will eat crops or wool. However, they are beneficial to night-blooming flowers who depend on moths for pollination.

CLASSIFICATION

KINGDOM: *Animalia*

PHYLUM: *Arthropoda*

CLASS: *Insecta*

ORDER: *Lepidoptera*

BLOOD THIRSTY

While most moths eat natural fibers and nectars, the vampire moth is a blood sucker! These moths use their proboscis (tongue-like member) to penetrate the skin of animals and humans. But don't worry, they do not pose a threat to humans.

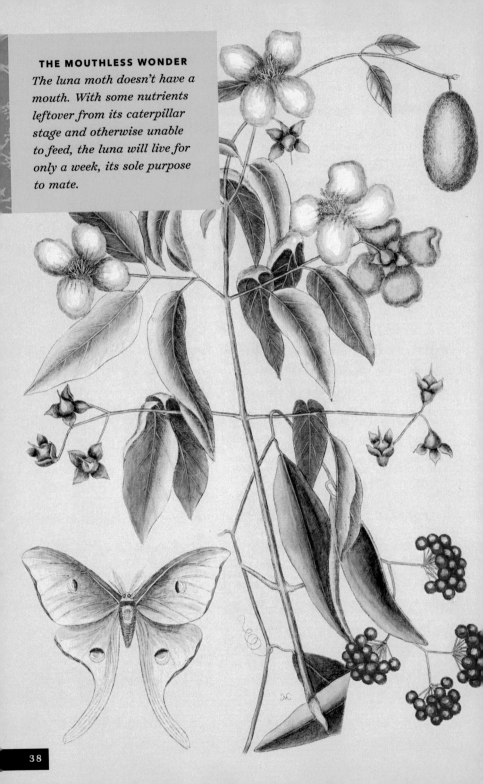

THE MOUTHLESS WONDER

The luna moth doesn't have a mouth. With some nutrients leftover from its caterpillar stage and otherwise unable to feed, the luna will live for only a week, its sole purpose to mate.

NIGHT VISION

Moths are nocturnal and use chemical senses to find each other at night. Some male moths can smell a single female from seven miles away.

7. TERMITE

While finding termites in your home is never good, they do make the *outside* world a better place. Termites play an important part as nature's decomposers by feasting on decaying wood. They also aerate the soil. They live in a caste system, with each caste having its own role to fill. While the king and queen termites are the only ones with eyes, all termites use their sense organs at the base of their antennae to understand the world around them. For instance, they can sense vibrations and then create vibrations of their own by banging their heads against tunnel walls to warn the colony of danger. One danger might be their number one predator: ants. The two insects are known to fight each other over food and territory.

KINGDOM: *Animalia*

PHYLUM: *Arthropoda*

CLASS: *Insecta*

COHORT: *Polyneoptera*

SUPERORDER: *Dictyoptera*

ORDER: *Blattodea*

INFRAORDER: *Isoptera*

FEAST OF FECES

Termites share an interesting bond: they eat each other's poop! As newborns, they don't have enough bacteria, so they fix this by eating feces. Gross!

2.

3.

6.b

7.a

8. FLEA

Fleas are amazingly athletic insects. With just a miniscule frame, they can lift 150 times their body weight. Parasites by nature, they consume fifteen times their body weight in blood daily. Their thin and smooth body allows fleas to move freely in the fur or feathers of their hosts. While they can't fly or run fast enough to reach a host, they *can* jump on one. In fact, fleas can jump 30,000 times without stopping and reverse their direction each time. Virtually blind and deaf, these insects prefer humid environments where they can lay eggs and populate quickly. It only takes twenty-one days for a single flea to turn into a swarm of 1,000 fleas. So keep your eyes open for fleas on your furry friends!

KINGDOM: *Animalia*

PHYLUM: *Arthropoda*

CLASS: *Insecta*

SUPERORDER: *Panorpida*

ORDER: *Siphonaptera*

DARK PAST

Millions of people died in Europe during the Middle Ages due to the Black Plague. The rapid spread of the disease came in large part from infected fleas that passed the illness from rodent to human.

PREHISTORIC PRESENCE

It's believed that dragonflies have been around for 300 million years. Prehistoric dragonflies are estimated to have had two-and-a-half foot wingspans!

9. DRAGONFLY

Adragonfly is a four-winged insect known for its bright colors and long abdomen. They can be found in warmer climates and like to live close to water. A distinguishing characteristic is their large compound eyes, which are made up of thousands of smaller eyes. This excellent eyesight aids in hunting. With nearly 360° vision, dragonflies can always see their prey and predators, even at a distance and no matter if flying forward or backwards. They even catch their prey and eat while in midair. Dragonflies are helpful to humans because they keep mosquito and gnat populations in check. One dragonfly can eat up to one hundred mosquitos every day.

CLASSIFICATION

KINGDOM: *Animalia*

PHYLUM: *Arthropoda*

CLASS: *Insecta*

ORDER: *Odonata*

SUBORDER: *Epiprocta*

INFRAORDER: *Anisoptera*

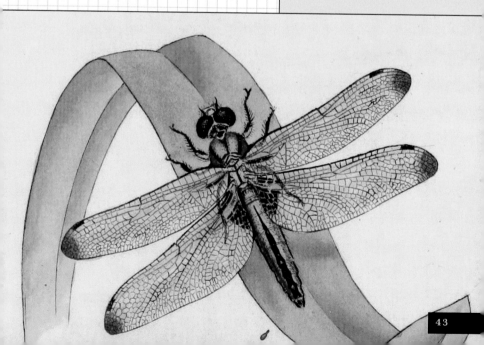

BEAUTIFUL . . . AND BIG

*Most dragonflies reach
two inches in length,
while the largest,
Megaloprepus, can grow
to be 4.7 inches in length
with an impressive 7.5-
inch wingspan.*

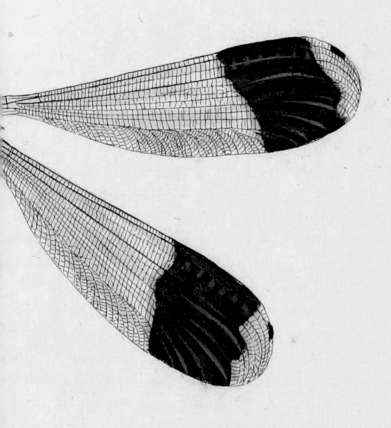

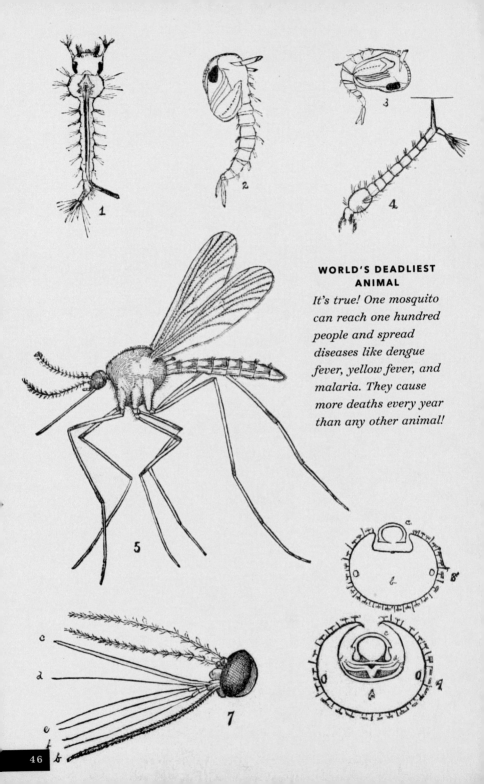

WORLD'S DEADLIEST ANIMAL

It's true! One mosquito can reach one hundred people and spread diseases like dengue fever, yellow fever, and malaria. They cause more deaths every year than any other animal!

10. MOSQUITO

Wherever you venture, unless you travel to Antarctica, you will find mosquitos. There are trillions of these pesky insects worldwide and over 3,000 species. While they do play an important role in the food chain as prey, mosquitos are, well, usually an unwanted visitor. Interestingly, only about 200 species feast on human blood—and it's only the females who do. Males, though they can still be annoying, are actually harmless. Mosquitos must lay their eggs in water, so it's best to empty any standing water around your home. While they don't have great vision, mosquitoes are attracted to the carbon dioxide you breathe out. Thanks to their olfactory receptors, they can find you up to thirty feet away!

CLASSIFICATION

KINGDOM: *Animalia*

PHYLUM: *Arthropoda*

CLASS: *Insecta*

ORDER: *Diptera*

SUPERFAMILY: *Culicoidea*

FAMILY: *Culicidae*

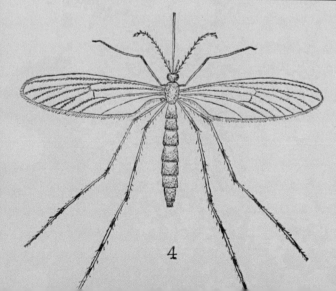

4

BUZZ OFF

That irritating sound mosquitos make? That's caused by the rapid beating of their wings. Mosquitos beat their wings 300-600 times per second. That's way faster than even a hummingbird.

47

SUMMER FLING

New colonies are started each spring by the queen wasp. As she lays eggs and the colony grows, the population can reach 50,000 wasps in summer.

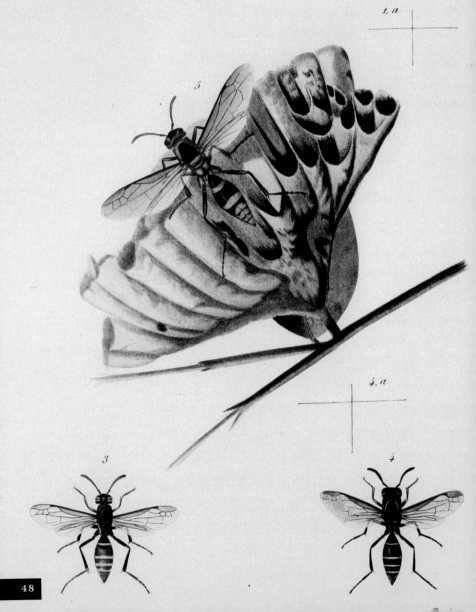

11. WASP

More aggressive and noisy than their honeybee cousins, wasps have the ability to sting repeatedly. They do have a productive and helpful side, though. Wasps feed on insects that cause harm to gardens, like aphids and grasshoppers. In fact, they are released by the thousands on farmland to help control crop pests. (How's that for a natural pesticide!) There are around 30,000 wasp species, and they can be found worldwide. Their slender, smooth bodies and bold coloring of black and yellow make them easy to identify, though they can come in red, orange, green, and blue, too.

CLASSIFICATION

KINGDOM: *Animalia*

PHYLUM: *Arthropoda*

CLASS: *Insecta*

ORDER: *Hymenoptera*

(UNRANKED): *Unicalcarida*

SUBORDER: *Apocrita*

WATCH OUT!
Yellow jackets are the most aggressive stingers among all wasp species. When cold weather comes, starvations hits, and yellow jackets grow aggressive as they look for food. They have been known to massacre entire beehives to take their food.

CREATIVE CONSTRUCTION
To build a nest, wasps first chew up strips of tree bark, add digestive enzymes, and then throw it all up. This process creates a malleable, papery pulp, which is the basic building material of all wasp nests.

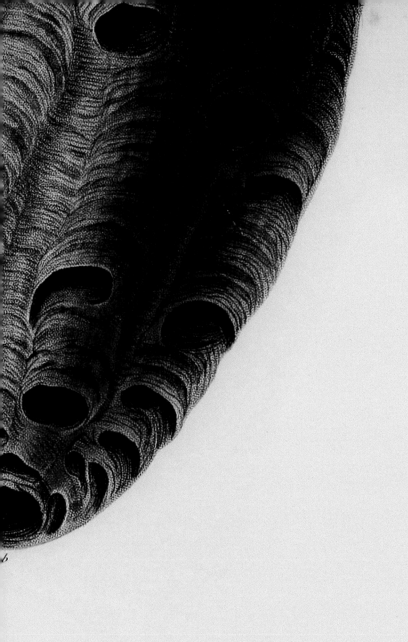

PLAGUE OF GRASSHOPPERS

Droughts are usually caused by prolonged hot, dry conditions—the same conditions grasshoppers thrive in. In extreme cases, what little crops might be left in a drought can quickly get consumed by the flourishing insects. Not a great combination.

12. GRASSHOPPER

Like all insects, grasshoppers have a head, thorax, abdomen, and six legs. There are over 11,000 species, and while they do come in the classic green color, grasshoppers can also sport a yellowish brown, reddish brown, or even striped exterior! Impressive jumpers, grasshoppers can sometimes get confused with crickets. You can tell them apart, however, since grasshoppers hear with their abdomen, eat only plants, and make noise by rubbing their forelegs against their wings (crickets rub just their wings together). They make a tasty meal for rodents, birds, and larger insects, but they can be destructive to human crops. When grasshoppers swarm together, they can leave farmers, and therefore people, without food by completely consuming the foliage in the fields.

CLASSIFICATION

KINGDOM: *Animalia*

PHYLUM: *Arthropoda*

CLASS: *Insecta*

ORDER: *Orthoptera*

SUBORDER: *Caelifera*

INFRAORDER: *Acrididea*

LONG JUMP CHAMPIONS

Grasshoppers can jump one meter in length, which is an incredible distance for their size. This would be the equivalent to a human jumping further than the length of a football field.

DINNER IS SERVED

If you are looking to try some new dinner recipes, you might want to try some protein-rich grasshopper dishes. You can roast, bake, or fry them. Enjoy them in tacos or purchase them dipped in chocolate!

Scientists believe grasshoppers have been around for
300 million years. We can still find the fossils of ancient
grasshoppers and occasionally the nymph stage of
grasshoppers preserved in amber (fossilized tree sap).

13. CRICKET

You've probably heard a cricket if you've listened to that familiar chirping noise in your backyard on a warm summer evening. In fact, each of the 900 cricket species has its own unique chirp, which it makes by rubbing special parts of its wings together. Generally, only the male crickets chirp, and he uses different tunes for attracting a mate than he does for warning other males to back off. Crickets can hear messages like these through the hearing organs on their legs. Male crickets chivalrously protect their mates—even if it costs their lives. With a short lifespan of less than a year, crickets thrive in warmer temperatures and can be found in rainforests, deserts, mountains, or marshlands.

KINGDOM: *Animalia*

PHYLUM: *Arthropoda*

CLASS: *Insecta*

ORDER: *Orthoptera*

SUBORDER: *Ensifera*

INFRAORDER: *Gryllidea*

SUPERFAMILY: *Grylloidea*

CRICKET CALCULATOR

Here's a crazy trick: you can calculate the outside temperature by tracking the number of cricket chirps you hear in a minute's time. Take the number of chirps in a minute, divide by four, and add forty.

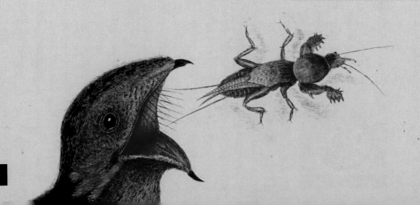

14. SILVERFISH

Silverfish are one of the most ancient insects alive today—they've been around for 400 million years! They also have a long lifespan (for insects). Under the right conditions, they can live up to eight years. Yet even after all those millions of years of hanging around, silverfish never did develop wings to fly. Maybe they don't need them, because these insects are *quick* on their feet. They move their bodies side to side to outrun their enemies, mimicking the movement of a fish (hence the name). You can find silverfish in their favorite habitat: places that are humid, damp, and dark. Silverfish hide in the day. At night, they're on the move looking for food. Since silverfish can chew, they especially enjoy sugars and starches—just like the ones found in book bindings, paper, and cereal.

CLASSIFICATION

KINGDOM: *Animalia*

PHYLUM: *Arthropoda*

CLASS: *Insecta*

ORDER: *Zygentoma*

FAMILY: *Lepismatidae*

GENUS: *Lepisma*

SPECIES: *L. saccharinum*

HARD TO KILL
As far as pests go, silverfish are some of the most resilient to insecticides. Because they've been around for so long, it's believed they have built up various tolerances to such chemicals.

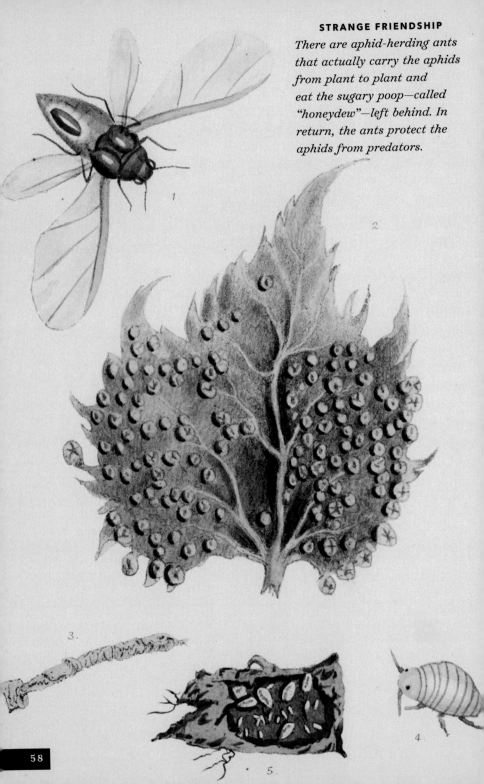

There are aphid-herding ants that actually carry the aphids from plant to plant and eat the sugary poop—called "honeydew"—left behind. In return, the ants protect the aphids from predators.

1

2

3.

4

5.

15. APHID

Aphids are tiny, sap-sucking insects that are pretty much found wherever there are plants. You can find them in large colonies on the underside of plant leaves. Aphids are usually wingless, plump, and slow moving. This makes them an easy target for predators like ladybugs and lacewings. Don't be fooled, thought, because these insects don't get eaten without a fight! Aphids will kick their predators with their hind legs, kill their enemy's eggs, or just roll off whatever plant they are on to avoid being eaten. While good at providing food to the food chain, aphid species number over 4,000 and are destructive to human crops. In a matter of seconds, they can transmit fatal viruses from a diseased plant to a healthy one.

WELL-KNOWN NAMES
Aphids have earned many nicknames over time. If you hear someone refer to "plant lice," "green flies," "ant cows," or "los afidos," you guess it: they're talking about aphids.

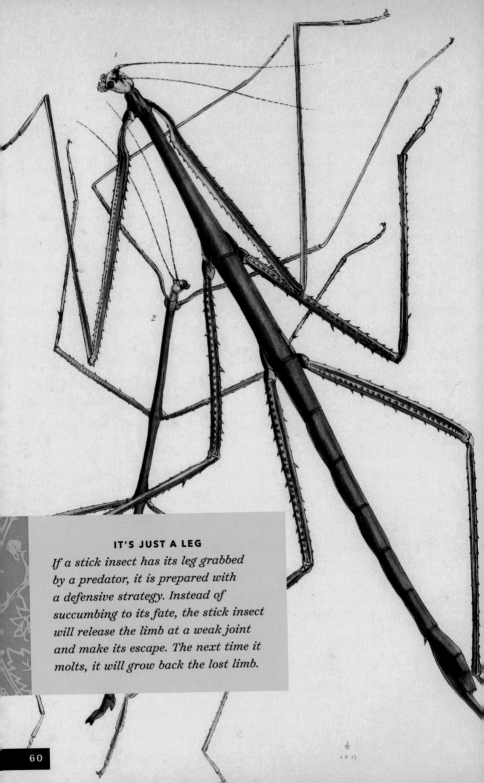

IT'S JUST A LEG

If a stick insect has its leg grabbed by a predator, it is prepared with a defensive strategy. Instead of succumbing to its fate, the stick insect will release the limb at a weak joint and make its escape. The next time it molts, it will grow back the lost limb.

16. STICK INSECT

Stick insects are some of the most interesting insects in the animal kingdom. You might hear them called "walking sticks" and "bug sticks," which makes total sense because that's exactly what they are. Masters of disguise, stick insects look just like the twigs and branches around them. They will even sway with the wind to look like they're a part of a tree. Mostly nocturnal, stick insects will stay still in trees during the day and feed on leaves after dark. While this is a beneficial safety strategy for stick insects, it is no match for bats. Night hunters, bats use echolocation to pinpoint these insects by their sound. Stick insects are found on all continents (except for Antarctica), with the largest numbers of the 3,000 species found in the tropics.

CLASSIFICATION

KINGDOM: *Animalia*

PHYLUM: *Arthropoda*

CLASS: *Insecta*

COHORT: *Polyneoptera*

MAGNORDER: *Polyorthoptera*

SUPERORDER: *Orthopterida*

ORDER: *Phasmatodea*

SUPER STICK
While it might be terrifying to run into one in the wild, the giant Chinese stick insect is an awe-inspiring sight! As the longest insect in the world, it can reach two feet in length.

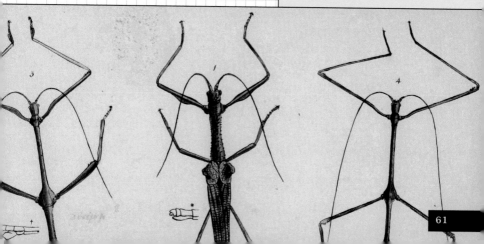

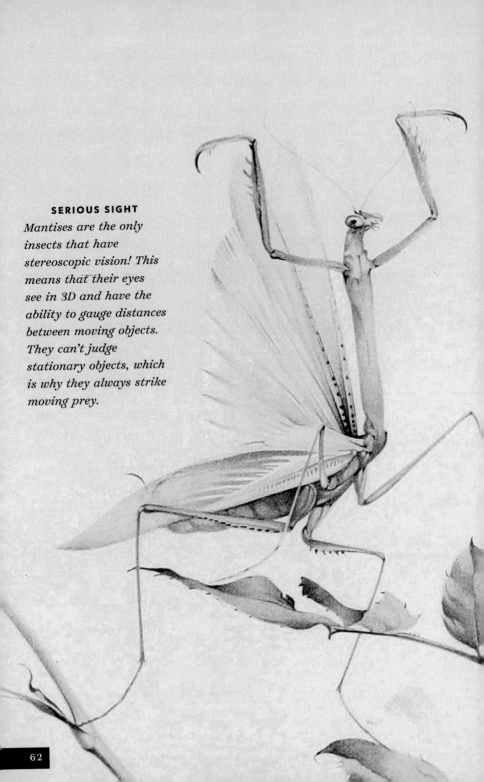

SERIOUS SIGHT

Mantises are the only insects that have stereoscopic vision! This means that their eyes see in 3D and have the ability to gauge distances between moving objects. They can't judge stationary objects, which is why they always strike moving prey.

17. MANTIS

Also known as the "praying mantis," the mantis's name comes from the Greek word *mantikos*, meaning "prophet." This is fitting, as a mantis's unmoving upright stance and folded arms gives the look of a person in serious prayer. Perhaps more fitting, however, would be the name "preying" mantis, because these are cunning hunters. Mantises have the ability to turn their heads 180°, which keeps them alert to their surroundings, and have sharp spikes on their forelegs, which aid in snatching their prey. But sight might be a mantis's greatest strength. With two large compound eyes on the sides of their heads for detecting light, and three smaller eyes in the middle for seeing movement and depth, nothing gets past a praying mantis! While most species reside in rainforests, you can spot these remarkable insects in grasslands, deserts, and other places with warmer climates.

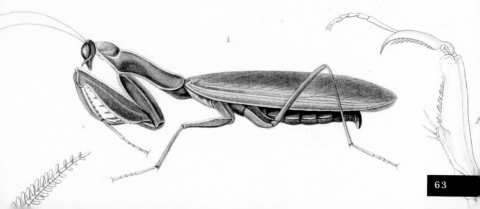

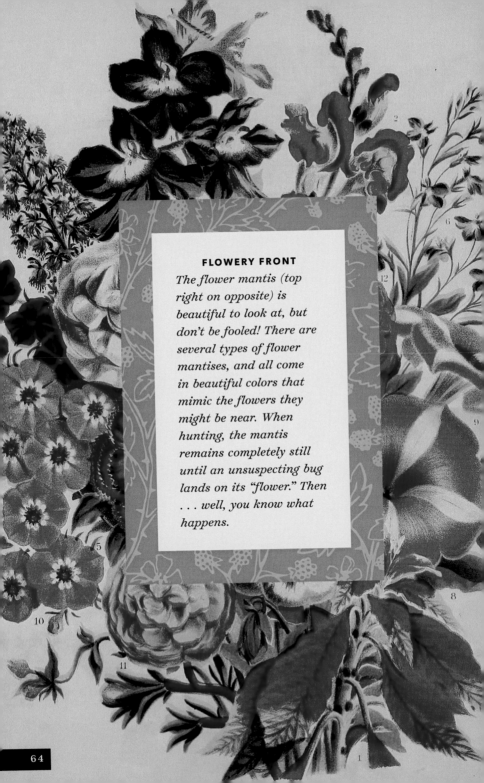

FLOWERY FRONT

The flower mantis (top right on opposite) is beautiful to look at, but don't be fooled! There are several types of flower mantises, and all come in beautiful colors that mimic the flowers they might be near. When hunting, the mantis remains completely still until an unsuspecting bug lands on its "flower." Then . . . well, you know what happens.

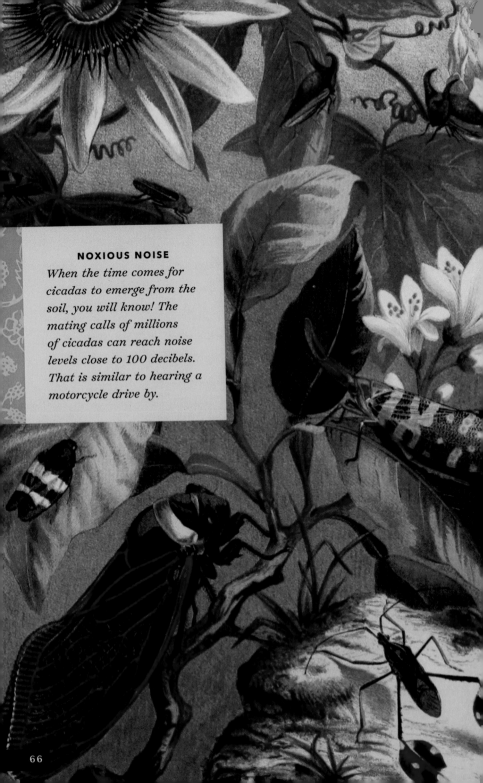

NOXIOUS NOISE

When the time comes for cicadas to emerge from the soil, you will know! The mating calls of millions of cicadas can reach noise levels close to 100 decibels. That is similar to hearing a motorcycle drive by.

18. CICADA

Part of the *Cicadae* family and making up over 3,000 species, cicadas are remarkably unique insects. There are two main types of cicadas: annuals, which are found worldwide in temperate climates, and periodicals, which are only found in North America. Periodical cicadas emerge in rhythmic cycles that occur every thirteen or seventeen years. After hatching, cicadas spend most of their lives as developing nymphs and feeding on liquid nutrition from tree roots. At the end of their life cycle, they come to the surface all at once in a synchronized fashion. Just one acre of land can be the emerging place of 1.5 million cicadas practically overnight!

CLASSIFICATION

KINGDOM: *Animalia*

PHYLUM: *Arthropoda*

CLASS: *Insecta*

ORDER: *Hemiptera*

INFRAORDER: *Cicadomorpha*

SUPERFAMILY: *Cicadoidea*

WINGED WONDER
The largest species of cicada insects is the Malaysian emperor cicada (shown below). With large black wings, a yellow-green collar, and a wingspan of up to eight inches, these insects are a showstopper!

LUCKY NUMBER 64

*How do cicadas know when to emerge? Scientists
believe it has to do with temperature. When the soil
at eight inches underground reaches exactly 64°
Fahrenheit, it is a signal to the cicada nymphs that it's
time to begin their upward climb to the surface.*

MOLTING MAGIC

When cicadas become adults, they molt and leave their old exoskeletons. You can find them left behind on the branches and trunks of trees.

IMPOSTERS

Trout and other fish love to eat mayflies. A clever fly fisherman knows to use fishing lures that resemble the local mayfly species and use flicking motions that imitate the movement of the insects.

19. MAYFLY

Mayflies are aquatic insects that are found near rivers and streams worldwide. They also go by the nicknames of "shadflies," "fishflies," and "Canadian Soldiers." With lengthy wings and long torsos, it's no surprise that mayflies are related to dragonflies and damselflies. Maylies have the shortest adult lifespan of any insect. After hatching, they enter the nymph stage, where they live up to a year in freshwater, feeding on decaying plant and animal matter. Once they reach adulthood, they will mate, spawn, and die—all within one day. Why so short? For one thing, adult mayflies don't have mouths or any way to consume food. In this way, they're rather similar to the luna moth.

CLASSIFICATION

KINGDOM: *Animalia*

PHYLUM: *Arthropoda*

CLASS: *Insecta*

SUBCLASS: *Pterygota*

DIVISION: *Palaeoptera*

SUPERORDER: *Ephemeropteroidea*

ORDER: *Ephemeroptera*

STANDARD SETTERS
Mayflies are often used to help determine the water quality of a river, stream, or lake, because they can only live in clean, unpolluted water. So if mayflies are around, it means the water is good!

ABOUT THE AUTHOR

Christin is the author of several books for kids. She lives with her family in California, where she enjoys rollerblading, puzzles, and a good book.

BUSHEL
& PECK
BOOKS

ABOUT THE PUBLISHER

Bushel & Peck Books is a children's publishing house with a special mission. Through our Book-for-Book Promise™, we donate one book to kids in need for every book we sell. Our beautiful books are given to kids through schools, libraries, local neighborhoods, shelters, nonprofits, and also to many selfless organizations who are working hard to make a difference. So thank you for purchasing this book! Because of you, another book will find itself in the hands of a child who needs it most.

Printed in the United States
by Baker & Taylor Publisher Services